MW01487767

Scholarships for

College Students

Tips to Help College Students Pay for College and Reduce Student Loans

Also by Marianne Ragins

Winning Scholarships for College
College Survival & Success Skills 101

Scholarships
for
College Students

*Tips to Help College Students Pay for
College and Reduce Student Loans*

Marianne Ragins

TSW Publishing
P. O. Box 176
Centreville, Virginia 20122
www.scholarshipworkshop.com
TSW Publishing is a division of The Scholarship Workshop LLC

ISBN: 978-1-950653-15-7

Printed in the United States of America

This book is available at special quantity discounts for bulk
purchases for sales promotions, premiums, fundraising, and
educational use. Special versions or book excerpts can also be
created to fit specific needs.

For more information, please contact
info@scholarshipworkshop.com or call 703 579-4245. You can
also write: TSW Publishing, P. O. Box 176, Centreville, Virginia
20122.

Dedication

To my mother, my husband and my children; your
love, motivation, and presence in my life keep me
going.

For G. L. Solomon
As one who truly got the most from life
and helped us to get the most from ours,
your sunny smile, loving heart and
generous ways will be remembered forever
by all of your family and friends.

CONTENTS

Introduction

As an author who writes about getting college money, a successful scholarship winner, and as a workshop leader, I frequently get asked if there are scholarships for current college students. The answer to your question is yes, there are definitely scholarships for students already in college. In some cases, students who are enrolled in a college or university have a better chance at winning certain scholarships, especially those that are college/university sponsored, mainly because of close proximity to the source of those scholarships. In addition, undergraduates and graduate students have numerous chances to get involved in organizations and associations affiliated with their majors that also sponsor scholarships. Often these associations have scholarships available. The National Society of Professional Engineers and the National Association of Black Accountants are two such organizations.

Also, when reading through any of the lists of scholarships in books, scholarship directories, or program websites, the additional eligibility guidelines will usually state whether a program is available to current college students. Some requirements may require enrollment in a two or four-year university or college.

So if you already started college and now realize you need or want more money to finish, review the following tips for ways to get additional funding for your education.

- Look for scholarships and awards as soon as you know you may need more money. Even if you don't need additional funding, you can apply for merit scholarships, which don't require you to have financial need. Merit scholarships can look great on your résumé or curriculum vitae and may help you amass a powerful network of mentors and fellow scholars. But be careful! Some schools may reduce your financial aid package if you win an outside scholarship. If this happens, contact your financial office immediately to discuss your options.
- Review books such as *Winning Scholarships for College,* 5th edition or later and directories such as the *Ultimate Scholarship Book* for sources of financial aid.
- Consider entering contests such as writing, photography, and beauty that offer monetary awards.
- Visit websites such as http://www.finaid.org, http://www.fastweb.com, http://www.scholarshipworkshop.com, and http://www.scholarships.com for information about scholarships and other college funding.

- Speak with your academic department to get information about sources of non-need and need-based funding for students in your major.
- Contact the alumni association for your school in your hometown and ask if they offer scholarships or financial aid to students currently attending the school. Many often do, yet the funds are not heavily advertised.
- Contact church/religious, civic, and community organizations in your hometown and where your school is located. Many will help students by offering additional funds to keep them in school. Some also have scholarship programs for students in or from the area.
- Check with your advisor on campus. They may be aware of funding opportunities available to you.
- See if you may be able to get work study in one of your school's on-campus offices.
- Research service scholarships for loan repayment or forgiveness possibilities. If you're willing to work for an organization either during, before, or after you graduate for a specified time period, you may be able to get help with outstanding student loans or current and future college bills. Organizations such as AmeriCorps and entities affiliated with the Public Service

Loan Forgiveness Program fall into this category. See www.studentaid.gov (search for Public Service Loan Forgiveness) or the chapter, "Scholarships and Awards for Volunteering, Community Service & Work" in the 5th or a later edition of *Winning Scholarships for College* for more information about these types of programs.

1

Understanding Free College Funding Options for College Students

Let's start with understanding the difference between searching for scholarships and free college funding as a current college student and as another student type. These include the search for funding in high school, as a transfer student, or even a nontraditional student. There are differences but also similarities in the search. For example, consider the situation for each of the following types of students.

- *For high school seniors*—scholarships may be more abundant, particularly small amounts in the community.
- *For college students currently enrolled*—undergraduate scholarships may not be as abundant, but you have the campus/community as a resource and can still search for funds based on your interests, major, or career goals.
- *For transfer students* (from a two-year/community college)—undergraduate scholarships may not be as abundant, but you have the campus/community as a resource and

can still search for funds based on your interests, major, or career goals. You also have the opportunity for transfer scholarships. Visit Phi Theta Kappa and see PTKConnect (http://www.ptk.org/ptkconnect) for an online search of institutions offering transfer scholarships.

- *For nontraditional students* — scholarships for adult students may also not be as abundant, but you still have the campus/community as a resource, just as currently enrolled students do. Nontraditional students should also revise their thinking. Don't just look for scholarships for nontraditional or older students. Remember! You are also an undergraduate student. Search for scholarships targeting adult students as well as those for college students or college undergraduates.

- *For all students* —look for scholarships based on who you are, where you are, what you are, and your interests. For example, many organizations, particularly those designed to serve a specific population (like women) could be an opportunity for you! So, if you are female, search for scholarships targeting women. Are you interested in culinary arts? If so, then search for scholarships targeting culinary arts. Are you a cancer survivor? If so, then search for scholarships intended for survivors of cancer.

As outlined above, you'll see there are many scholarships available, intended for all types of people. You just need to spend the time and expend the effort to find them.

2

Going Beyond Assumptions

Review eligibility requirements carefully. A scholarship program may mention student classification but not age. For example, a scholarship directory or database entry may look like this one.

Create-A-Greeting Card Scholarship
Website: www.gallerycollection.com (*Search for Scholarship Contests*)
Amount: $10,000

- To qualify to receive a scholarship award, you must:
  - Be a high school student (at least 14 years of age or older), college student or members of the armed forces enrolled during the time-period of the contest in an academic program designed to conclude with the awarding of a diploma or a degree.
  - Create a design for a Christmas card, holiday card, birthday card or all-occasion greeting card.
  - Be a legal resident of the fifty (50) United States, the District of Columbia, American Samoa, Guam,

the Commonwealth of the Northern Mariana Islands, the U.S. Virgin Islands, or Puerto Rico.
o   International student who has a student visa to attend school in the United States.

In the example listed above, the eligibility requirements do not mention age. The example only mentions qualifications as they relate to your status in an academic program, your status or as resident in the US or its territories and your willingness to create a design for a greeting card.

Entries in scholarship and award directories might also include a category showing target applicants. For example, the entry might include a section such as this one:

Target Applicant:

- College student
- Graduate student
- Adult student

Once again, the entry above does not mention age, only classification. As a result, if you are a currently enrolled college student or a community college student transferring to a four-year institution, reviewing directories that include entries with target applicants such as the one above could uncover several scholarship sources for you.

As a student already enrolled in college, review the next section and the checklist for additional sources of financial aid at the undergraduate level.

3

Associations and Other Membership Organizations Can Help

To find associations and organizations in your area of study and check to see if any of them offer scholarships, look at the *Encyclopedia of Associations* published by Gale Research, which can usually be found at your local library. You can also use web search portals such as Google to search for organizations in your field. I used one of them to conduct an advanced Internet search for engineering societies and associations and found quite a few that offer scholarships. In the area of engineering, there were at least four organizations that offered scholarships. They included the Minerals, Metals and Material Society, the American Ceramic Society, the Association for Iron & Steel Technology and the American Society of Mechanical Engineers. All of these organizations offered some type of engineering scholarship to students already enrolled in college. Likewise, an advanced search for physical therapy associations and societies yielded the American Physical Therapy Association (APTA). This association for physical therapy recognizes outstanding students pursuing this occupation with the Mary McMillan Scholarship Award.

To conduct an advanced search, visit an advanced search page on an engine such as Google (https://www.google.com/advanced_search). Then see the following chart to review how to conduct an advanced Internet search for specific terms. For this search I wanted to find engineering societies that might have scholarships. So, I entered the terms shown on the chart below and uncovered three engineering societies which included the National Society of Professional Engineers. You can also be more specific with your search to find certain types of engineering scholarships.

Advanced Search		
Find Results	all of these words	engineering
	the exact phrase	Society
	any of these words	Scholarship
	none of these words	

Be aware that membership can definitely have its privileges. Some associations may require you to be a member of their organization to be eligible for a scholarship. If so, the membership fee is usually reduced for currently enrolled students.

See the following for our suggestions to help you uncover opportunities offered by membership organizations such as associations and honor societies.

- <u>Membership organizations</u> - If you are a member of any organization on campus or in your community, contact the organization to determine if scholarships or general college funding is available to members. Your church or faith based organization is one example. Another example is the NAACP, a community based civic organization, that has scholarships available to its members and others. You should also contact your parents about organizations of which they may be members, since some organizations may have scholarships available to their members' children.

- <u>Scholastic Honor Societies</u> - Honor societies such as Golden Key International Honour Society (http:/ /www.goldenkey.org) or Phi Theta Kappa (http://www. ptk.org) and many others have scholarships available to their members. There are hundreds of scholastic societies that cover interest areas from music to chemistry and beyond.

- <u>Associations</u> - Associations are a wonderful resource for students of all ages in the scholarship process to explore. There are thousands of associations in the United

States. Moreover, many of them have scholarships available to students who want to continue their studies and pursue a career in their field or interest area.

4

Finding Hidden Gems to Finish Your Education

Explore the following areas for additional options to help you fund your continued college education.

- Digital or print versions of magazines directed toward career and success-oriented people, such as *Kiplinger's Personal Finance*, *Black Enterprise*, and *Fortune*.
- Try to get a paid internship. Many corporations sponsor internship programs for undergraduates and graduates. Some will also sponsor scholarships for interns who have performed well academically. Even if they do not fund all or part of the education of an intern, the job experience will enhance your résumé for future employment and scholarship consideration.
- Contact the athletic office if you participate in any type of sport. Athletic scholarships can be offered for many different athletic activities such as swimming, lacrosse, and tennis. To get a sports scholarship, you don't always have to play football, basketball, or baseball.

- Contact the financial aid office at your college or university. Read your college or university catalog for a list of fellowships, endowments, and scholarships to get an idea of money you might qualify for. You should also visit the financial aid section of your school's website. It's good to have an idea of the school's available student aid funds so you can ask specific questions about money to help you finish your education.
- If you participate and have a serious interest in activities such as music, dance, theater, or art, contact those departments to see if scholarships are available in those areas.
- Review directories that list grants in specific areas to see if there might be aid opportunities that could apply to you. For example, check out the online directory Foundation Grants to Individuals by Candid (https://grantstoindividuals.org) or The Foundation Directory Online by Candid at https://fconline.foundationcenter.org). You may also be able to review an older edition of this directory in your local library.
- See if you are eligible for an out-of-state tuition waiver if you attend a public college or university out of your home state but in a neighboring state.

- Try to get a company to sponsor you in exchange for your endorsement of its products or services.
- Consider cooperative education. With this option you may alternate attending school with extended periods of work for a company or agency that needs students in your area of study. This period could last from several months to a year. The company or agency you work for generally pays your tuition bill, or provides a salary designed to cover your tuition, in exchange for your services. In this arrangement your school may also give you academic credit based on the work experience you are accumulating in your field while working with the company or agency. Learn more about cooperative education and internships which are similar in *College Survival & Success Skills 101*. See www.scholarshipworkshop.com for more information.
- Contact honor societies in your area of study.
- Check out companies in need of future employees in your area of study or a related area.
- Check with organizations that benefit certain groups to which you belong (for example, legally blind, women, minority, etc.).

- Contact alumni associations, particularly in the city you're from, for scholarships. Contact the national alumni association office for your college or university as well.
- Contact your state financial aid agency or state grant agency.
- If you attend a United Negro College Fund (UNCF) college or university, see http://www.uncf.org for information about numerous scholarships that may be available to you.
- Explore crowdfunding. If you have a compelling story about why you need money to begin or complete your education, crowdfunding sites allow you to attract people over the Internet who are willing to donate to your cause. GoFundMe.com is a popular crowdfunding site used by many.
- Contact professionals who are already working in the field you are planning to enter. Ask if they know of associations or organizations that could help you complete your education. For example, if you're studying in the field of veterinary medicine, contact a veterinarian. Alternatively, if it's anthropology, contact an anthropologist. Doing so may or may not help you find a scholarship opportunity, but it could get you a paid internship and/or valuable work experience that can help you win scholarships, grants, or open doors to other

opportunities. You should do this in addition to trying to find national associations and organizations that may be listed in a book or online, because professionals in your area may know of smaller, community and regionally based organizations that offer support to students. On social media sites such as Facebook or Twitter, search for associations that are affiliated with your field. For example, you can input "marketing associations" into the search bar and see if any promising organizations come up. Reading a few Tweets or glancing at the Facebook page will give you an idea of whether it may be helpful to you in your search.

5

Federal and State Funding for College Students

Help from the government comes in a variety of forms. For instance, you can obtain grants and loans from the United States government. Or you can get help from the government as a taxpayer with certain tax credits for educational expenses. The Lifetime Learning Credit and the American Opportunity tax credit are two credits of this type that are explained later in the chapter. State governments also participate heavily in contributing to the students of their states by offering various types of aid programs ranging from tuition waivers to full scholarships.

For federal and some state assistance you will need to complete the Free Application for Federal Student Aid (FAFSA). The FAFSA will help most colleges and universities to determine your financial aid package. As a current college student, you've hopefully completed this process. You should complete the financial aid forms which are usually required by your college or university whether you think you have financial need or not. The financial aid package usually contains some type of federal aid such as the Pell Grant, work-study, or a Direct or Plus Loan, in addition to university scholarships. For some institutions, you will also need to complete the CSS–Financial Aid PROFILE (College Scholarship Service–Financial Aid PROFILE). You may also have to submit another financial aid form specific to the institution you are planning to attend to determine your aid package.

For information about the CSS PROFILE, visit www.collegeboard.org. To get more information about the federal financial aid forms, visit the following web sites and social media platforms:

Federal Student Aid and Free Application for Federal Student Aid (FAFSA)

Website: https://studentaid.gov/h/apply-for-aid/fafsa
Facebook: https://www.facebook.com/FederalStudentAid
Twitter: @FAFSA
YouTube: http://www.youtube.com/user/federalStudentAid

Federal Student Aid Handbook

Website: https://fsapartners.ed.gov/knowledge-center/fsa-handbook
Facebook: https://www.facebook.com/FederalStudentAid
Twitter: @FAFSA

YouTube:
http://www.youtube.com/user/federalStudentAid

IRS Tax Information and Benefits for Students

Website: http://www.irs.gov/Individuals/Students

Now let's answer a few basic questions that will help you understand the financial aid process and how it works. If you have questions about the process at your specific college or university, visit the financial aid office as soon as possible.

What is a Financial Aid Package?

A financial aid package is the total amount of financial aid a student receives. For example, a package could consist of loans, grants, work-study (work-study is a job arranged for you on the college campus and funded by the federal government as part of your financial aid package to assist with college expenses), and scholarships. The contents of a financial aid package are usually communicated to a student in a financial aid award letter or an electronic communication. As a current college student, you should already know the available aid being offered to you by your institution each year as long as you've completed the appropriate forms.

How is a Financial Aid Package Determined?

A financial aid package is determined primarily by the FAFSA, and/or the CSS-Financial Aid PROFILE and the financial aid committee/director at your college or university. Both the FAFSA and the CSS-Financial Aid PROFILE are financial aid forms with several differences that help to determine a student's total need. The FAFSA uses federal methodology to determine your need and the CSS-PROFILE uses institutional methodology and may be requested by some private colleges and universities.

What is My Financial Need?

The amount of financial need you have will be based on how much you and your parents can contribute to the total cost of your education at the college you attend. The amount you and your parents can contribute plus the amount of outside aid you will receive (such as scholarships that are not from the university or college to which you are applying) is subtracted from the total cost of college attendance to obtain your total need. Your contributions will be based on your current income, assets, etc. To get an estimate of your need and expected family contribution, and for an idea of how much federal financial aid you may be able to receive, visit the federal student aid information web sites provided to you at the beginning of the chapter.

Once need has been demonstrated and is sent to the college on your student aid report (SAR), your institution will determine your total financial aid package and the amount of your need they can meet. Some colleges and universities meet 100% of your need. Some don't even come close. It depends on your institution and the circumstances. You should also keep in mind that if you have been awarded a financial aid award package by a specific college or university and you win an additional merit based non-need scholarship award, your financial aid package at the school may be reduced. It may be reduced because the additional award lowers your total need amount. For example, if your financial aid package at a school is for $15,000 per year and you win a scholarship for $5,000 a year, your award package at the school may be reduced to $10,000 per year. If you win a need-based award, but have already received a financial aid package from your institution meeting your total financial need you may be ineligible to receive this award even after you've won it, since the award amount can never be higher than your actual need. Some schools will allow you to use the additional monies towards books and personal expenses. Ask your college about their policies regarding this issue. Also, some scholarship programs will work with you on this as well. So if you've won a scholarship and you think you may not be able to use it, contact the scholarship program to let them know. They may be able to suggest additional options.

Explore each of the following sections to find sources of aid to assist you with your continued education. Some are mentioned in earlier sections but here's a quick summary:

- Federal aid - Visit the Federal Student Aid section on the Department of Education's website (http://www.ed.gov) to determine if you are eligible for any federal aid or grant programs.
- State aid - Find the organization in your state designated to administer funds for students who are residents of the state. For example, in Virginia, this organization is the State Council of Higher Education for Virginia (SCHEV). To find the education agency for your state, visit https://www2.ed.gov/about/contacts/state/index.html. If this page is no longer available, search the Internet for "state higher education agency." You may want to also perform an advanced Internet search and include a search for your state as well to get specific results. See the chapter, "Strategies for Using the Internet," for assistance with conducting an advanced Internet search.

Steps for Appealing a Financial Aid Decision or Requesting an Adjustment/Reconsideration

If you are unhappy with the amount of financial aid being offered by your institution, consider asking for an additional aid. This is often called an adjustment. Following are steps you can use to request more financial aid from your college or university in addition to finding additional college funding from outside sources.

Step 1

Review your financial aid award carefully and consider the following:
- Has anything changed about your financial situation since you completed the financial aid form?
- Is there an impending change that will affect your finances? (i.e. birth of a child, another dependent)

Step 2

Gather any documents needed to support your claims above. This should include income statements, expense records, and recurring or major bills.

If you are interested in additional aid because another college is offering more money, obtain a copy of your award letter from the other school and include it with your supporting documentation. You should also support your appeal with clearly articulated reasons for why a school is your first choice and why you may have to accept the other school's offer because your family cannot afford your first choice with the current aid package offered.

Step 3

How should you contact the financial aid office? If possible, visit or call the office and request an in-person appointment. As a current college student, visiting the office on campus to see someone immediately or to request an appointment should be easy. If that is not possible, you should send a detailed letter via certified mail with documents to support why you believe your aid package should be adjusted. You should make sure to alert a specific financial aid administrator with whom you have already briefly outlined your situation, that a letter will be coming to their attention. Don't just send your letter randomly.

Step 4

Even if your aid package is not adjusted initially, there may be an opportunity months or weeks after your appeal. For example, if you approach a school about work study and they don't have anything available at the time of the appeal, this does not mean they will not have work study later. Or they may be able to steer you towards another on-campus position.

Tax Assistance for College Expenses

The government also provides aid in the form of tax credits, which can help ease the burden of college expenses. Some of the major tax credits and deductions are explained in the following:

The American Opportunity Tax Credit

This credit is for qualified education expenses paid for an eligible student for the first four years of higher education. Eligible students can claim up to $2,500 for expenses on tuition, fees, and educational materials in the first four years of post-secondary education. This credit is dependent upon your filing status and income level. See publication 970 at http://www.irs.gov or your tax professional for additional information. Low-income families who owe no tax may also be eligible to receive a credit refund of up to $1,000 for each qualifying student.

The Lifetime Learning Tax Credit

This tax credit focuses on adults who want to go back to school, change careers, or take a couple of courses to upgrade their skills. It is also applicable for students who are already in college such as juniors, seniors, graduate students and professional degree students. Using the Lifetime Learning credit, a 20% tax credit can be taken for the first $10,000 of tuition and required fees paid each year. For example, a secretary, whose family has an adjusted gross income of $60,000, wants to attend a graduate program at a public university ($2,700 tuition). Her intention is to upgrade her skills to get a management position eventually. The secretary has been working and out of college for the past 12 years. If she uses the Lifetime Learning credit, her family's income taxes could be cut by as much as $540. The Lifetime Learning tax credit is available for tuition and required fees minus grants, scholarships, and other tax-free educational assistance. See publication 970 available at www.irs.gov or your tax professional for additional information.

Coverdell Education Savings Accounts

If your parents started a Coverdell Education Savings Account in your name when you were under age 18, money can be withdrawn to pay for post-secondary tuition and required fees (less grants, scholarships, and other tax-free educational assistance), books, equipment, and eligible room and board expenses, and no taxes will be due. Once you reach age 30, the Coverdell Education Savings Account must be closed or transferred to a younger member of the family.

Early Withdrawals from IRA's

Do you or your parents/guardians have an IRA? Generally, when you withdraw money from an IRA before your reach age 59 ½ you are subject to an additional 10% tax on the money withdrawn. However, if the money is withdrawn to pay the qualified higher education expenses of you or a dependent in that year, the additional 10% tax will not be owed for the early withdrawal. See www.irs.gov (publication 970) or your tax professional for additional information.

Tax Free Interest for Education Savings Bonds and Employer Provided Educational Assistance

Normally, interest earned on savings bonds and money provided by your employer to pay for your higher education is taxable. However, the interest earned on certain types of bonds that are cashed in and used for the qualified higher education expenses is not taxable. Your ability to take advantage of this assistance will depend upon your income level and marital status. Likewise, your employer can provide you with up to $5,250 each year for higher education without including this amount in your taxable income. See www.irs.gov (publication 970) or your tax professional for additional information.

Lowering the Overall Cost of Your Student Loan

If you are currently repaying student loans, you may be able to take a deduction for interest paid on

Scholarships for College Students

your student loans. The deduction is available even
if you do not itemize other deductions. The
maximum deduction is $2,500. It is phased out for
certain income levels. See www.irs.gov (publication
970) or your tax professional for additional
information. The deduction is available for all loans
taken to pay tuition or other qualified higher
education expenses.

For additional information about other tax
assistance or deductions, please visit the IRS web
site at www.irs.gov and read or download IRS
Publication 970. You can also call 1-800-4FED-AID.

6

Scholarship Research for College Students

Your search should include the following three areas:

- The library
- Local sources: the local search should involve searching for funds available in your community, state, and region.
- The Internet (covered in the next chapter)

For a comprehensive search that gives you the best and most opportunities to win scholarship money, devote close attention to all three!

Library Search

To start your scholarship journey, you should go to the nearest library. Once there, do the following:

- Look for scholarship directories such as the *Ultimate Scholarship Book*.
- Search for books such as *Winning Scholarships for College* that go beyond the standard listing found in a scholarship directory. The focus for books of this type is to help you learn how to win scholarships. As a result, they may have limited listings

but each listing would include as much additional information on winning the scholarship as possible.

- Search for newspaper articles about scholarships. Newspapers such as *USA Today* periodically have articles about getting money for college. To find articles in sources like these as well as the magazines above, use the library's online database or microfiche. In addition, an Internet resource you can use would be Google Alerts.

Local Search

The local search is one most often ignored by the typical student. Usually someone searching for scholarships uses a few scholarship directories and an Internet search service such as www.fastweb.com or www.scholarships.com. For some students in search of college money, an Internet search service is the only resource used. Although search services similar to www.fastweb.com can be wonderful, you should not ignore other sources to find funding. If your scholarship quest includes directories and the Internet only or even just the Internet, you could be overlooking some valuable scholarship opportunities.

The best way to have a complete scholarship search is to search locally in your community, state, and region as well as using directories and the Internet. Most of the scholarships you find in directories and on the Internet are national which means that if you apply, you are among many others who hope to win the scholarship. This makes winning the scholarship harder because it is more competitive. For many local scholarships the number of applications received from students is much smaller which makes them less competitive. This is probably because local scholarships are generally smaller in monetary value and a lot of students feel they aren't worth the time and effort. Fortunately smaller, easier to win scholarships, do add up and should definitely not be ignored. In my scholarship total of more than $400,000, awards as small as $50.00 were included.

For a local scholarship search, you should do the following.

- Search for community foundations. Visit the Northern Virginia Community Foundation (www.cfnova.org) for an example of a community foundation and to see types of scholarships a community foundation might have. Visit the Internet search section of this publication to learn how to conduct an advanced search for scholarship information.

- Research local clubs and organizations. Examples of these would be the Soroptimist Club, the Optimist Club, Exchange Clubs of America, Daughters of the American Revolution, YMCA/YWCA, the Kiwanis Club, the Rotary Club, the Lions Club, or the Knights of Columbus. Also look for sororities and fraternities. Executive Women International, an organization that has local clubs throughout the country, has a scholarship program for "past high school age" and nontraditional students already enrolled in college.

- Contact companies and banks located in your community. Some may have scholarships available to local residents. Call the personnel/human resource or marketing departments of these companies to inquire if they offer scholarships to students in the community.

- Check with your employer. Some employers will pay for the continuing education of their employees. This includes starting or completing a college or graduate degree.

- If you belong to a work-related union, contact the union to find out if they have scholarships available to their members. Union Plus is an example of a union that maintains a scholarship program for members and their families.

- Contact any organization to which you or your parents belong, local or national, to determine whether they have a scholarship program for their members. Your church or faith related organization might be an example.

- Since some credit unions have scholarship opportunities for their members, you should also contact your credit union, if you have one.

7

Strategies for Using the Internet

You can use the Internet in many ways to get college information and find the money to pay your way. The example listing in this resource gives you a general summary for many types of programs. If the web page you would like to view is no longer available, try an advanced search on Google because the location may have changed. Or, the competition may have been suspended or discontinued due to lack of funding or a new direction. Unfortunately, this can happen at any time with any program. To help stay informed about new programs, join The Scholarship Workshop on Facebook (www.facebook.com/scholarshipworkshop) or follow us on Twitter @ScholarshipWork and Instagram @ScholarshipWorkshop for information about new scholarship programs.

Using General Search Engines

- Visit search engines such as Yahoo!, Ask, Bing, and Google. Search for terms such as, "college scholarships," "financial aid," and "scholarships." Each of these search engines will give you a list of websites and articles where the term you searched for is included. This will lead you to specific scholarship program websites.

- You can also use general search engines to find out if an organization you have heard about in the news or elsewhere has a web address. For example, if a news article lists a program, put the entire name of the program into the search box of an engine with quotation marks around it. By doing this, you may be able to go directly to their website if the search engine finds a link. Or use Google Alerts (www.google.com/alerts) to get e-mail alerts for recent articles written about scholarships, college, and financial aid.

Advanced Internet Search

Have you ever entered a search term in the main search box of a general search engine and received millions of results or advertising pop-ups that really aren't relevant? An advanced search will help you cut through the clutter. You can use the advanced search function in a general search engine such as Google or Yahoo! to find specific information for your scholarship search. An advanced search helps narrow the results you might get from an Internet search.

Perhaps you want to find a scholarship for students in their freshman year of college, The example below shows the information you might include for this type of advanced search. Inputting this information into the Google Advanced search uncovered the *Leaders Save Lives Scholarship* offered through the Red Cross. This opportunity is available to all college students willing to sponsor a

Scholarships for College Students
community blood-draw event. You could do a similar search for "sophomore, junior or senior" or "college sophomore" as your exact phrases.

Advanced Search		
Find Results	all of these words	scholarship
	the exact phrase	undergraduate
	any of these words	freshman
	none of these words	

Alternatively, you may want to find scholarship essay contests, awards, or prizes that are not based on need. See below for an example of this type of advanced search. Conducting this advanced search can uncover millions of results for essay contests. You could even narrow the results further based on your state or city to find essay-based scholarships near you. Also, to eliminate expired competitions, include the current year as well.

Advanced Search		
Find Results	all of these words	scholarship
	the exact phrase	undergraduate
	none of these words	need
	any of these words	essay or prize or contest

Another possible type of advanced search is one based on finding merit or achievement-based scholarships. Merit or achievement scholarships often do not have a financial need component. See below for entries to include for this type of search. For exact phrase, input "merit" to search for merit-based scholarships. For another search, input "achievement" for the exact phrase to search for achievement-based scholarships.

Advanced Search		
Find Results	all of these words	undergraduate scholarship
	the exact phrase	merit
	none of these words	need
	any of these words	award or prize or contest

Lastly, another type of scholarship you can search for is one based on submitting a video in a competition. These generally do not have a financial need requirement either. What would this type of advanced search include? Take a look below for an example.

Advanced Search		
Find Results	all of these words	undergraduate scholarship
	the exact phrase	video
	none of these words	need
	any of these words	award or prize or contest

8

Finding Scholarships Specific to You and Your Family

You should make an effort to find scholarships specific to you and your family. Although some of the opportunities you find may have a need-based component, others do not. You can start exploring specific scholarships by asking yourself the following questions:

What are your hobbies?

There are many scholarships for people who have particular hobbies. Books with extensive scholarship listings will have special sections dealing with these types of scholarships. Look for these special sections during your scholarship search. Some scholarship directories will title this section as extracurricular activities. An example of a scholarship or award that focuses on your hobbies would be the Pokémon World Championships (https://www.pokemon.com/us/play-pokemon —see *World Championships*). Players can win up to $25,000 in scholarships or cash.

If you are currently employed, where do you work?

Contact the personnel or human resources office of your employer to inquire about scholarship opportunities and tuition reimbursement programs. If your company does not have a personnel office, speak with the general manager about the possibility of scholarship opportunities, or contact the company's general headquarters to learn if such opportunities exist. Many companies offer tuition reimbursement programs as an employee benefit. In tuition reimbursement, the employee initially pays the cost of tuition and fees for the courses taken in college or graduate school. Once the courses are completed and a satisfactory grade has been earned by the employee, the company/employer will then reimburse all or part of the tuition and fees initially paid by the employee. Some companies pay these costs upfront. As a student working at Wendy's Old-Fashioned Hamburgers in high school, I was eligible for a Wendy's scholarship which I applied for and won. Likewise, McDonald's also offers tuition assistance to employees through *Archways to Opportunity*, a program to help pay for college courses taken at an "approved school" such as an accredited two or four-year public or private college or university; business, technical or vocational school; or graduate or post-graduate school.

For what company or companies do your parents currently work?

Ask your parents to contact their company personnel or human resources department to inquire if there are scholarships available to the children of employees. If the company does not have a personnel office, your parent should speak with the general manager about the possibility of scholarship opportunities or contact the company's general headquarters. Scholarship directories also list companies that sponsor scholarship programs for the children of their employees. You can also check books or online directories such as *Foundation Directory Online* (https://fconline.foundationcenter.org/welcome/quick-start), to learn whether your parent's company has a foundation set up to disburse scholarship money to the children of their employees or for other purposes. For example, Johnson Controls, Inc., maintains the Johnson Controls Foundation that offers scholarships to its employees' children. Alternatively, conduct an advanced search using the "company name" and the word "foundation" as your search queries.

Do you belong to a religious organization; for example, a church or synagogue?

Many religious organizations give scholarships not only to members of their congregations but to nonmembers as well. Some of them stipulate that the recipients of their scholarships must attend a college or university established to operate under the edicts of their denominational faith, such as a Presbyterian college or university. An example of this type of scholarship would be the Presbyterian Scholarships (http://www.presbyterianmission.org) offered to students who are members of the Presbyterian Church and are planning to attend a college related to the Presbyterian Church (U.S.A). Contact churches and religious organizations to inquire about scholarships such as these. You can also look in scholarship directories for the sections based on religious affiliations. In addition, speak with the minister of the church that either you and/or your parents attend. Most churches are more than willing to establish a small scholarship fund for their students. For instance, the church I was a member of in Macon, Georgia, Stubbs Chapel Baptist Church, gave me a small scholarship to attend college and also gave me money every year while I was enrolled.

Are you a child or close relative of a war veteran? If so, in which war and in what branch of service did your relative serve?

Numerous scholarships are available for children and close relatives of veterans who served in specific wars, such as World War II. Books with extensive scholarship listings will have special sections dealing with these types of scholarships. The sections may be titled "Armed Forces" or "Military." You will need to know the branch of the Armed Forces in which your relative served to find scholarships that apply specifically to you. Examples of these scholarships are those offered by the Military Benefit Association, which provides scholarships to its members who serve in the military (http://www.militarybenefit.org). The Fisher House Foundation's website (http://www.militaryscholar.org) is another resource for scholarship information associated with the military.

Are you a veteran or a disabled veteran?

Scholarship and financial assistance is available to most disabled veterans, especially from the government. If you are a disabled veteran, contact the Federal Student Aid Information Center (800-433-3243), visit StudentAid.gov to inquire about scholarship opportunities, or call the Department of Veterans Affairs (800-827-1000; http://www.va.gov or http://www.gibill.va.gov). You may find governmental organizations with programs that pay for tuition, fees, books, and equipment of veterans disabled during active duty and honorably discharged. To find financial aid such as this, look in the "Military Disabled" or "Armed Forces" sections of scholarship guides such as the *Ultimate Scholarship Book*

Are you legally blind or do you have any other disabilities?

Students who are legally blind or in some other way disabled can usually receive scholarships and financial aid assistance from many sources, especially the government. During your search, look for directories that have special sections dealing with scholarships for the disabled. The American Council of the Blind (http://www.acb.org)

currently offers scholarships to students who are legally blind.

Are you related to someone with a disability or who is a survivor of a disease?

For example, if your parent is deaf or hard-of-hearing, the Millie Brother Scholarship for Hearing Children of Deaf Adults is offered through Children of Deaf Adults (CODA) (www.coda-international.org). There are also scholarships for survivors of certain diseases such as cancer. Currently the Dr. Angela Grant Memorial Scholarship Fund awards scholarships to cancer survivors or those within the immediate family of a cancer survivor (http://www.drangelagrantscholarship.org). This is an area where an advanced Internet search, could be helpful to you in finding college aid specific to your situation, disease, or disability.

For minority groups other than African American, can you trace your lineage? (For example, Samoan, Japanese, Native American, etc.)

Many programs have scholarships strictly for minorities of a certain descent. To win these scholarships you may be required to prove your lineage. Look for scholarships such as these if you fall into this category. An example of this type of scholarship would be the scholarships offered by the Welsh Society of Philadelphia to students of Welsh descent (http://www.philadelphiawelsh.org). To be eligible to receive this scholarship, applicants must prove their lineage and enroll in a college within

100 miles of Philadelphia. Similarly, students who have Asian Pacific Islander heritage and can describe ethnicity, heritage, or ancestry in relation to the countries, territories, or lands in Asia or the Pacific Islands can qualify for the Asian and Pacific Islander Americans (APIA) scholarship program (https://apiascholars.org).

Are you or your parents a member of a union, trade group, or association?

If you or your parents are members of a union, trade group, or association, you may be eligible to win scholarships such as the E. C. Hallbeck Memorial Scholarship offered by the American Postal Workers Union (http://www.apwu.org) to high school seniors who are dependents of active or deceased members of the union. Or consider the scholarship program from Union Plus (http://www.unionplus.org), an organization established by the AFL- CIO to provide consumer benefits to members and retirees of participating labor unions.

What are you strongly interested in studying at college?

Scholarships are available to students interested in a particular major. If you are certain of your intended major, look for directories and scholarship opportunities in that area. For students interested in the field of health care, for example, the Tylenol Future Care Scholarship program (https://www.tylenol.com/news/scholarship) is available, or consider reviewing scholarships offered by the American Medical Association Foundation (https://amafoundation.org/programs/scholarships). The scholarships don't just stop at health care or medicine—you can find other associations for scholarships in other fields. Use a scholarship directory or perform an advanced Internet search to find scholarships related to your current or future major. Another great resource you can use is the "Field of Study Index" in *Scholarships, Fellowships and Loans* published by Gale Research. This resource may be found in your local library.

Are you a member of a fraternity or sorority?
Many sororities and fraternities sponsor scholarships. For instance, members of Theta Delta Chi can apply for scholarships, and the Alpha Kappa Alpha Sorority, Inc., Educational Advancement Foundation also offers several scholarships, including some that are open to nonmembers. As you look through scholarship directories, look for scholarships sponsored by a fraternity or sorority. If you are unable to discover any, write or call the national chapter of your organization, or visit its website, Facebook, or other social media platforms to uncover opportunities. In fact, local sororities and fraternities will often contact me (author of this book) to help them advertise a scholarship program that may be suffering from a low application rate.

Are your parents' members of a fraternity or sorority?
Some sororities and fraternities sponsor scholarships for the children of their members. As

you look through scholarship directories such as the *Ultimate Scholarship Book,* look for scholarships sponsored by your parents' fraternity or sorority. If you are unable to discover any, write to the national chapters of the organizations or visit their website, Facebook, or other social media platforms, if available. You can also do an advanced Internet search.

Are your parents' alumni of a college or university?

Many colleges and universities offer scholarships to the children of their alumni. Contact the college or university they attended to inquire about scholarship opportunities that may be available to you.

Where do you live? Have you checked for community foundations in your area?

Numerous scholarships are offered by organizations and companies to students who live in a specific area, usually where the company or organization is located or does business. To find scholarships in this category, do an advanced Internet search to find community foundations, county websites, or school websites with scholarships specific to your area. Use search terms such as "scholarships" and the name of your county, city, or state to find scholarships in local areas. Also do the same for "scholarships" and the search words "community foundation" along with the name of your city, county, or state to uncover community foundations in your area. For example,

the Community Foundation of Northern Virginia
(https://www.cfnova.org), the Berks County Community
Foundation in Pennsylvania (http://www.bccf.org), and
the Community Foundation of Central Georgia
(http://www.cfcga.org) are all examples of community-
based foundations that serve a specific community
or a group of communities within a specific region.

What are your extracurricular activities?

Activities such as participation in Distributive
Education Club of America (DECA;
http://www.deca.org), Future Business Leaders of
America (FBLA; http://www.fbla-pbl.org), National
Society of Collegiate Scholars (NSCS; https://nscs.org)
and Phi Theta Kappa (PTK; https://www.ptk.org) may
allow you to become eligible for scholarships from
these organizations or as members of these
organizations. For example, members of DECA at
the collegiate level are eligible for corporate
sponsored scholarships in various areas.

9

Scholarship Jumpstart for First Year College Students and Beyond

There are also opportunities for new college freshmen and students currently enrolled in college to obtain additional funding to continue or complete their education. These include various types of scholarships, grants, prizes and awards. See below to get an idea of the opportunities available and to get started on your college funding journey today!

A FEW IMPORTANT ITEMS TO REMEMBER

- Do not rely solely on the following scholarship list. It is best to use the strategies described throughout this book to uncover the most opportunities available to you.

- Some programs change their application requirements and eligibility guidelines. Please review their websites carefully for any changes.

- Programs can and do stop awarding scholarships or suspend their scholarship programs. Don't get discouraged. You can still find available scholarships. But please know that there are no guarantees about the availability of a given scholarship, or that you will win it.

- Follow us on Facebook (http://www.facebook.com/scholarshipworkshop), Twitter (@ScholarshipWork) and Instagram (@ScholarshipWorkshop) for frequent alerts on new scholarships and upcoming deadlines. Join our mailing list to get the latest updates about scholarships and other helpful information. See https://scholarshipworkshop.com/newsletter to join.

The Christophers Annual Video Contest for College Students

Website: https://www.christophers.org/video-contest-for-college-students
Additional Information: In this yearly contest, students enrolled in undergraduate or graduate college classes, full or part time, can create a film or video (5 minutes or less in length) to communicate the message and mission of The Christophers and the belief that one person can make a difference. Any genre or shooting style is acceptable and must be submitted for upload onto the contest site or as a link. Prizes range from $100 to $2,000.

College JumpStart Scholarship

Website: www.jumpstart-scholarship.net
Additional Information: This scholarship is open to 10th through 12th grade high school students, college students and non-traditional students who are U.S. citizens or legal residents. You must be attending or planning to attend an accredited 2-year, 4-year or vocational/trade school in the U.S. and be committed to using education to better your life and that of your family and/or community.

College Is Power Scholarship

Website:
http://www.collegeispower.com/scholarship.cfm

Additional Information: This scholarship is available to students 17 years of age or older who plan to start a program of higher education within the next twelve months or who are currently enrolled in a program of higher education. You must be a full- or part-time student, attend a campus-based or online program and be a citizen or permanent resident of the United States. Award amount is $1,000.

Collegiate Inventors Competition

Website: http://www.invent.org (see *Collegiate Inventors*)

Additional Information: This competition recognizes, encourages, and rewards students to share their inventive ideas with the world. To compete, you must be enrolled full-time or part time in any U.S. college or university. You can enter as an individual or in a team of up to four people. Your entry must be your original idea and product. See website for complete entry requirements. Awards vary up to $10,000. Although not technically a scholarship, cash prizes can be used however you choose including paying for college.

Create-A-Greeting Card Scholarship Contest

Website: www.gallerycollection.com/greetingcardscontests.

htm or www.gallerycollection.com/greeting-cards-scholarship.htm

Additional Information: This $10,000 scholarship contest is open to all high school AND college students who are enrolled during the time-period of the contest in an academic program designed to conclude with the awarding of a diploma or a degree. To participate, applicants must create a design for a Christmas card, holiday card, birthday card or all-occasion greeting card. Legal residents of the fifty (50) United States, the District of Columbia, American Samoa, Guam, the Commonwealth of the Northern Mariana Islands, the U.S. Virgin Islands, and Puerto Rico are eligible to enter. International students who have a student visa to attend school in the United States are considered legal residents and are also eligible to enter.

DoSomething.Org Easy Scholarship Campaigns

Website: http://www.dosomething.org (see *Scholarships*)

Additional Information: DoSomething.org is a nonprofit for young people focused on social change for causes such as bullying, homelessness, and cancer. To apply for a scholarship, you need to complete a campaign and prove it with pictures of you in action during the campaign. They have many campaigns featured on the website. The scholarship program is open to U.S. citizens 13 to

25 years of age and does not require a minimum GPA, an essay or recommendation.

Dr. Pepper Tuition Giveaway

Website: https://www.drpeppertuition.com
Additional Information: Students between the ages of 18 and 24 can win up to $100,000 in this giveaway by submitting a 1-minute video explaining their goal. Submitted videos are judged as winners based on the following:

- How you want to make an impact with your degree/education
- Inclusion of Dr. Pepper (not mandatory, but recommended)
- Impact the tuition prize could have on your life, your community, or the world
- Overall presentation quality

Frame My Future Scholarship Contest

Website: http://www.diplomaframe.com (search for "Frame My Future Scholarship Contest") or https://www.diplomaframe.com/contests/frame-my-future-scholarship.aspx
Additional Information: This contest is open U.S. citizens enrolled in community college, undergraduate, or graduate school attending a U.S. college or university full-time in the current academic year. To qualify, you must submit an original creation of poetry, photography, ink,

collage, painting, mixed media, or graphic design to share what you want to achieve in your personal and professional life after college. Students can win up to $6,000. Finalists are judged based on their entry and description. Winners are ultimately chosen by online vote. For additional information and current deadline, visit the website.

HOTH SEO Scholarship Program

Website: https://www.thehoth.com/seo-scholarship
Additional Information: HOTH is offering current college students and high school seniors accepted to an accredited university an opportunity to win a $1,000 scholarship. To enter, students must write an essay with a minimum of 1000 words on the topic of, "How Companies Can Take Advantage of Digital Marketing." For more details, visit the website.

Live Más Scholarship

Website: https://www.tacobellfoundation.org/live-mas-scholarship
Additional Information: The Live Más Scholarship is open to college students who submit a video between 30 seconds and 2 minutes in length that addresses these questions:
* What is your passion and how are you currently pursuing it?

Scholarships for College Students

- How do you plan to use your passion to uniquely make a positive change in your community or the world?
- How will your education help enable you to pursue your passion and make a change?

You must be between 16 and 26 years in age and on-track to apply for or enrolled in an accredited post-high school/post-secondary educational program (including accredited two-and four-year colleges, universities, vocational-technical and trade schools)

"Leading the Future II" Scholarship

Website: http://www.scholarshipworkshop.com
Additional Information: The "Leading the Future" Scholarship is designed to elevate students' consciousness about their future and their role in helping others once they receive a college degree and become established in a community. It is open to high school seniors or current college undergraduates who are U.S. residents. Visit the website to apply online.

MPOWER Scholarships

Website: https://www.mpowerfinancing.com/scholarships
Additional Information: MPOWER scholarships include the Monthly Scholarship Series, MPOWER Global Citizen Scholarship, Women in STEM Scholarship, and the MPOWER MBA Scholarship

Each specific scholarship can be from $1,000 to $10,000. Students become eligible for an MPOWER scholarship if they meet the following criteria:

- Accepted or enrolled in a full-time degree program at a U.S. or Canadian school that MPOWER supports. See website for lists of schools that MPOWER supports.
- An international student or DACA student permitted to legally study in the U.S. or Canada
- Able to meet any additional criteria outlined for specific scholarships

OppU Achievers Scholarship

Website: https://www.opploans.com/scholarship
Additional Information: Founded in 2016, this scholarship provides $2,500 for the current or future education costs of high school students and students who are enrolled at least part time in college, graduate, professional, or trade school. Applicants must also have a cumulative GPA of at least 3.0 on a 4.0 scale and submit an essay that tells the organization in 500 words or fewer, why you're an achiever. For example, can you answer yes to any of the following questions: Have you created opportunity for yourself? How have you created opportunity for others? Did you start a small business? Are you the founder of a community program? How did you overcome the odds and make your dreams—or the dreams of others—come true?

Scholarships for College Students

Project Yellow Light Scholarship/Hunter Garner Scholarship

Website: http://projectyellowlight.com

Additional Information: High school and college students who want to encourage fellow students to develop safe driving habits can enter the Project Yellow Light scholarship competition. Your entry, which will consist of a video, billboard design or radio spot designed to motivate, persuade, and encourage your peers not to drive distracted, can win you up to $8,000 for your education. The winning video may be turned into an Ad Council PSA that will be distributed nationally to 1,600 TV stations. The winning billboard design may be displayed on Clear Channel Outdoor digital billboards across the U.S. and the winning radio spot could be shared on iHeartRadio's national network. Visit the website for additional details and requirements.

Scholarship America Dream Award

Website: https://scholarshipamerica.org/students/browse-scholarships/apply-for-the-dream-award/

Additional Information: The Scholarship America Dream Award is for students who have completed at least a year of college. Dream Award scholarships can be in amounts from $5,000 to $15,000 per year and are renewable for up to three years. This scholarship is available to students at least at least 17, who have a U.S. high school diploma (or equivalent) and have completed at least one year of college, trade or technical school. You must be a U.S. citizen, U.S. permanent residents (holders of a Permanent Resident card), or an individual granted deferred action status under the Deferred Action for Childhood Arrivals program (DACA).

Scholastic Art & Writing Awards

Website: http://www.artandwriting.org
Additional Information: This program is designed to recognize outstanding talent among students in the visual arts and creative writing. Students submit individual works as well as art portfolios and writing portfolios for this competition. Check the website for entry details in the fall. Awards range from $1,000 to $12,500.

Shawn Carter Scholarship

Website: https://shawncartersf.com/scholarship
Additional Information: All high school seniors, students with GED diplomas, college undergraduates at two year or four year institutions, and students at vocational or trade schools who are 25 years old or younger can apply for this scholarship. You also need to be a U.S.

citizen and have at least a 2.0 GPA. See website for additional details.

Sodexo Foundation

Stephen J. Brady STOP Hunger Scholarships
Website: https://us.stop-hunger.org/home.html or http://www.sodexofoundation.org (see *Grants and Scholarships*)
Additional Information: Stephen J. Brady STOP Hunger Scholarships are open to students in kindergarten through graduate school (ages 5 to 25) who are enrolled in an accredited educational institution in the United States. The scholarships are available to students who have performed unpaid volunteer services impacting hunger in a community within the United States at least within the last 12 months. Additional consideration is given to students working to fight childhood hunger. A Community Service Recommendation may be required for this application form so ask recommenders (who must not be family members) for their recommendations early.

10

Using Crowdfunding for Additional College Funding

Crowdfunding allows students to tell their story over the Internet to thousands of people quickly and with minimal effort. Individuals all over the world with access to the Internet see a student's words and hopefully become compelled to contribute with funding. There are several popular crowdfunding sites such as www.gofundme.com or www.gogetfunding.com.

Following are some tips for a successful crowdfunding campaign:

- You should have great visuals. If you can take a picture of yourself with something from your college or university, like a sign or mascot, it might help to encourage alumni and others to donate because it may give them an immediate visual connection with you.

- Use social media. Let others know about your campaign on your social media accounts but ask ALL of your family members with active social media accounts to share. If you attend a church or faith based organization, ask them to share on their social media. Also contact the youth and young adult ministry, scholarship ministry, education ministry and similar ministries to let them know about your campaign.

- Don't forget to create a hashtag specific to your campaign. This can make it easier to follow your campaign and see the interest it's getting.

- Check with your current or future university to see how you can connect with alumni via social media, email, or another way to share your campaign. Also check out the website and social media accounts for the alumni association in your hometown.

- Give a compelling and interesting name to your campaign. It should be something that people can easily remember. For example, Amy Needs Your Dollars for College - I Could Be Your Future Physician.

- Post updates. Let people know how it's going for you. Share success and failure. And let them know how much you appreciate the money already contributed and how wonderful it will be when you reach your campaign goal. You might also share what you've done with money contributed so far.

- Offer an incentive. You could offer something like a free hour of live or web based tutoring for one student at the local high school or middle school for every $100 or $1,000 you receive. Or you could offer to spread the love by helping at a food bank, a shelter or some other community organization one hour per month every time you reach a $1,000 threshold (or some other number) in your campaign.

- In your story, share your future career plans and how you plan to help others in the future just like donors will hopefully help you now. For example, you could discuss setting up a mentoring program or joining an organization such as Big Brothers Big Sisters once you graduate. Or for those with family members affiliated with a Greek organization mention future participation in the community service efforts of those organizations (if you successfully pledge).

- Let donors know exactly how the money will be used. For example: I need $5,000 for my room and board deposit at XYZ university. Or you could indicate you need $5,000 to help pay next year's tuition and fees.

- Consider adding a video to your story. Something memorable would be best. People love videos with animals. Maybe include your favorite pet in a video saying how much you will miss him or her doing their favorite stunt while you're away at college. But you're planning for a great future for both of you in your own home after you graduate. Or perhaps the video could be of you showcasing a special skill or talent you plan to share with others as a future college student or graduate.

Crowdfunding is a great way to raise cash for school. However, your funding campaign may not raise as much as you want or need. You should make every effort to explore additional sources of funding explained in other sections of this chapter. Also don't forget to explore scholarships, grants and awards for current college students. Don't stop looking for additional funding until all your current and future college bills are fully funded.

11

Applications

For many scholarship programs administered or offered by foundations, associations, societies and other organizations, downloading applications from websites and applying online is very popular. Many students prefer applying online because it's quicker and easier. Unfortunately, it's also very easy to make mistakes and to give answers, especially short essay answers, that don't reflect a lot of thought.

To showcase your best self with an online application, follow these guidelines:

- If possible, print online applications first without completing them
- Complete them on paper
- Then transfer your answers from paper to your computer in the online application
- Print the completed application
- Proofread
- If you like everything and have no mistakes, press SEND or whatever button you need to press online to send the application. If you can, make a PDF copy of the applications you complete. This can make it easier to review your application to get ready for a potential interview.

12

Standing Out With Your Scholarship Application

What are winning elements? Winning elements are items that set you apart from the crowd. Review the following sections for examples of these winning elements.

Essays

Essays are very important to your winning a scholarship. An essay is where you can really shine and tell those who read it how you feel about a particular issue. An essay can help you to elaborate on activities you've outlined in your résumé/activity list. In fact, incorporating your activities, how they have helped to make you into the student or person you are, and how these activities may have helped others, are important features to include in an essay and make its content come alive for the readers, while showing your best qualities.

Your Work Samples

If you have done anything extraordinary or award-winning or that has received some type of recognition, include a sample as part of your application package. For example, in my scholarship search, I included an award-winning layout from the high school literary magazine where I was the editor. I also included poetry that had won awards as well. In one of my applications, I even included a poem I had written titled, "I Am a Child." I liked the poem and thought it represented my writing style and how I felt about life. It also coincided with my essay where I had written about using my journalism skills (gained through my extracurricular activities) to overcome poverty and destruction in America. The poem which had this line, "I am a child yet I have seen cruelty in the face of kindness," fit the theme of my application essay. For the essay, I had to answer the question, "You are at your 30th high school reunion. The president of the United States is part of your class. Yet, you are the guest of honor. Why?"

Make sure you don't go overboard when including samples of your work as part of your application package. One or two items you feel are appropriate are enough. Don't send anything that won't fit in a 9" X 11" envelope. And most importantly, if you are asked NOT to send anything extra, DON'T.

Articles

These articles could be on you or your activities (even if the article doesn't mention your name specifically). If you have been a part of an activity or if you started an activity that has been written about in your local newspaper or college newspaper, include a copy of the article. Some students might send a link but judges don't often have an opportunity to click on a link while reviewing an application. Once again, don't go overboard. One article, if you're also sending samples of your work is enough. Two articles should be your maximum if you're not including samples of your work.

Résumé/Activity List

Your extracurricular activities, leadership positions, community involvement, and your being a well-rounded student are very important to winning scholarships. To show your involvement in an organized manner with a résumé or an activity list closely resembling a professional résumé helps scholarship programs and educational institutions see your participation and leadership as a whole unit rather than scattered among a few lines on an application.

One of the best ways students can set themselves apart from others is through their extracurricular activities, especially with those that are community service based. Many organizations are very impressed by students who are involved in the community and in their school or educational institution. To show your involvement in an organized and impressive way, you can include a résumé or activity list with your applications. Although most applications will ask you about your activities and include lines for you to list them, your activities look better when presented as a whole and in a résumé-like format. Some students are using the word processing wonders available today to make beautiful résumés complete with pictures and graphic elements that anyone would be proud to show in a job interview. That's the idea. It's great if you have a scholarship judge looking at your résumé/activity list and not only being impressed by what you've done but also how you presented it. Just make sure you don't overdo it with pictures and graphic elements. Content is the most important factor.

STUDENT RÉSUMÉ EXAMPLE

Once you have uncovered the scholarship and free aid opportunities that are available to you, know that students who are enrolled in colleges and universities are expected to be more professional than high school students in their speech, manner of dress, and especially in presenting a résumé to an organization for a part-time job, internship, or a scholarship. To help you present your list of achievements and qualifications, the following résumé is an example of one I used as a college student in the 1990's. When you are applying for a job or an internship, include a one-page résumé. If you are applying for a scholarship to a scholarship committee, you can include a multiple-page résumé unless there are specific requirements you need to follow. Also, if you are a junior or senior in college, you may not want not to include high school activities unless they are particularly noteworthy or you wish to show a long-standing interest in a particular area. For example, if you are applying for a journalism scholarship you would want to show that your interest and focus in this area has been concentrated for a number of years.

One Page Résumé Example

Marianne N. Ragins

University Address	Permanent Address
FAMU Box 00000	P.O. Box 176
Tallahassee, Florida 32307	Centreville, Virginia 20122
Telephone: (904) 555-1234	Telephone: (703) 579-4245

Objective: Effective utilization of my extensive literary, analytical, and organizational skills for a major business entity

Education: Presently matriculating as a junior at Florida Agricultural and Mechanical University's School of Business and Industry.

Major:	Business Administration	
Expected Graduation:	April 1995	
Grade Point Average:	3.88/4.0	

Relevant Course Work: Honors English I and II; Principles of Economics I and II; Legal Environment of Business; Principles of Marketing; Intermediate Accounting I and II; Managerial Accounting; Quantitative Methods for Business Decisions I; Financial Accounting

Achievements: Winner of more than $400,000 in scholarship awards; cover story, *Macon Telegraph*, May 2 and 4, 1991; national headlines, Associated Press, May 3, 1991; cover story, Parade magazine; featured in *Essence*, *Newsweek*, *Money*, *Jet*, *Reader's Digest*, *People*, *Black Enterprise*, and YSB magazines; appeared on *Good Morning America* (ABC), *The Home Show* (ABC), *Teen Summit* (BET); January 11 declared Marianne "Angel" Ragins Day in Wilmington, Delaware; Dean's List—Fall Quarter 91/Spring Quarter 92/Fall Quarter 92/Spring Quarter 93; Coca-Cola Scholar; Armstrong Scholar; Wendy's Scholar; National Dean's List 1991-1993; Outstanding Service Award 1991; Letter of Commendation from Thomas B. Murphy, Speaker of the House, Georgia General Assembly 1991; Letter of Commendation from Clarence Thomas, Supreme Court Justice 1991.

Organizations: Presidential Scholars Association; Phi Eta Sigma National Honor Society; University Honors Council; volunteer coordinator for Special Olympics 1991; volunteer speaker for local area middle and high schools; Red Cross volunteer; Coordinator, *Benjamin D. Hendricks Undergraduate Honors Conference* 1993 and 1994; panel speaker, *The 21st Century—Education Beyond the Classroom* 1993; Mock Trial Team, Florida Collegiate Honors Conference 1992; Southern Regional Collegiate Honors Conference 1991; international speaker at the Crystal Palace, Nassau, the Bahamas 1993; Director of Organization and Planning, *Hometown News*; coordinating manager, *Close-up*.

Publications: Author and publisher (first and second editions) of *Winning Scholarships for College: The Inside Story*; national publisher for third and future editions, Henry Holt and Company, Inc., New York.

Work Experience:
06/93 to 08/93
EDS Belgium N.V.— *Overseas Internship Assignment in Brussels, Belgium*
- Assistant for the Sales, Finance, and Government divisions of EDS
- Extensive involvement with the preparation of financial documents and sales presentations

08/92 to 08/92
Electronic Data Systems (EDS)—*Internship Assignment in Raleigh, North Carolina*
- Proposal Manager:
- Entailed managing and editing material from proposal and technical writers, coordinating staff meetings and project deadlines, as well as overseeing all aspects of production concern- ing the submission of EDS' proposal for the Tallahassee Integrated Public Safety System.
- Proposal Team Staff Member
- Desktop publishing, word processing, and production for various proposals

Computer Proficiency: WordPerfect, Lotus 1-2-3, Ventura Publisher, Microsoft Word, MacDraw, Microsoft Excel, Microsoft PowerPoint, ABC Flowcharter, Photostyler, Freelance Graphics, Lotus Notes

References Available Upon Request

Also, you could organize your résumé in the following manner.

Departmental Clubs/Activities
Here list all activities you are involved in within your school

- *Student Government Association – 2022 to present*
List activity and years in which you participated
- *Greek Council – 2023* **List any positions of leadership held and year held as a subheading **
- *Future Business Leaders of America – 2022 to present*

Honorary Clubs
* List all organizations that you have been inducted into because of outstanding performance *

- *Phi Beta Kappa – 2023*

Community Clubs/Service Activities
List clubs or activities within the community

- *Role Models and Leaders Program – 2022 to present*
- *Macon City Volunteer Youth Coach – 2021 to present*
- *NAACP – 2023 to present*
- *Circle K International – 2022 to present*
- *Susan G. Komen Race for the Cure – 2022 to present*
- *Community Church Young Adult Group – 2023 to present*

Work/Internship/Research Experience

- *Laura's Babysitting Services – 2022 to present*

Awards/Honors
*List all the awards you have won.

- *Volleyball Team's Most Valuable Newcomer – 2023*

- Certificate of Participation – Core Advisory Day – 2022
- President's Student Service Award – 2022

*Items in italics <u>and</u> small type are notes to help you create your own résumé.

You can find other types of résumés in *Winning Scholarships for College*. Different formats are acceptable as long as your résumé is easily readable and well-presented.

Recommendations

Another area where students can stand out from the crowd is through the recommendations of others. In order to get the best recommendations, you need to be careful about who you ask, how you ask, and when you ask. Here are a few tools to help you do that.

First, consider the scholarship you are applying for. Even if the program is not requesting a recommendation, include one anyway especially if the recommendation is a good one or it highlights your community involvement. On the other hand, if a program specifies no additional documentation be included with your application, respect their wishes.

Nearly all scholarship programs are impressed by those with community involvement. If the program is requesting a recommendation, try to get at least one from an individual that fits the nature of the scholarship. For example, if it's for a STEM (Science, Technology, Engineering and Math) type of scholarship, get your physics, chemistry or another professor in a related field to write one.

In general, you should get recommendations from the following if you can:

- a professor
- an advisor, counselor, or administrator
- a coordinator for a community-based activity
- your minister or another clergyman if you have one
- anyone other than a relative who can discuss your most impressive qualities in a written format.

As you think of people to include on your recommendation resource list, make sure to include a sentence about they how they know of you. This will help you to pick and choose individuals to write recommendations as you begin applying for multiple scholarships. Also, when pondering who you should ask, think about whether the person is accustomed to writing recommendations for students or if they might be a good writer. If they have never written a recommendation and/or they aren't a good writer, your recommendation could be a nightmare or a "one liner."

When you ask for a recommendation, do the following:

- Give a written description of the scholarship and/or program
- Include your résumé and any extras you plan to send with your scholarship application

- Include a self-addressed stamped envelope with two stamps (if the recommendation needs to be sent in the U.S. mail)
- Ask at least four weeks before deadline
- Follow-up to see how they are doing or if they need additional information
- Send thank you notes or e-mails (if necessary – handwritten notes are more memorable). You may have to ask again.
- *Winning Scholarships for College* (5th or later edition) includes a sample letter requesting a recommendation as well as an example recommendation chart to help you keep track of recommendations and their due dates.

13

Essay Writing Strategies to Help You Win

For most essays, you can use the following five paragraph format particularly if writing is difficult for you. If writing is one of your strengths, there is no need to follow the five-paragraph format. Just make sure your essay is interesting and includes details about your extracurricular activities and/or your life. Also, make sure you actually address the answer to the essay prompt or question.

I. INTRODUCTION - ONE PARAGRAPH

- Use a quotation, poem, thought, amazing fact, idea, question, or simple statement to draw your reader into your topic.
- The main idea does not have to be stated in the first sentence, but it should definitely lead to and be related to your main idea or thesis statement, which should introduce three main points you will develop in the body of your essay.
- Avoid using statements such as, "I am going to talk about . . . " or "This essay is about . . ."

II. BODY - THREE PARAGRAPHS

- Support the main idea with facts, thoughts, ideas, published poetry, quotes, and other intriguing, insightful material that will captivate your audience.
- Present clear images.
- If necessary, use a thesaurus to ensure that you are not using the same words repeatedly. Using a word over and over will become monotonous for your audience and distract them from your subject.

III. CONCLUSION - ONE PARAGRAPH

- Restate the main idea in an original way.
- You can again use a poem or quotation to leave an impression. However, avoid using this tactic in all three parts of the essay. It may appear repetitious and unoriginal.
- Refer to the future in terms of your plans pertaining to the subject of your essay. For example, in an essay describing your future career goals, refer to yourself in the career that you have outlined. This reference should project you, and the ideas you presented in the essay, into the future.

* Special Note - Using quotations or poems can show that you are well read. If your essay looks like a dumping ground for quotes and the words of another, using quotations and poems could show something else entirely. Be selective and look for quotes that are enlightening and profound.

As you become more experienced with writing essays you can expand on the format by including more paragraphs or even reducing the number of paragraphs and abandoning the format. If you start with the basic five paragraph format, it is easy to adapt and change to fit the style of your essay, as I did when I wrote an essay for the Coca-Cola scholarship which had nine paragraphs. I also changed the format to write an essay for another scholarship program that had only two paragraphs. You can read both essays and an analysis of each in Chapter 11 of *Winning Scholarships for College*. Also consult *The Scholarship and College Essay Planning Kit* for additional essay examples and analyses.

Early in your scholarship search prepare two basic essays following the format above. The essays can easily be tailored later to fit most scholarship application essay requirements. Since many essays require descriptions of you and your future career goals, let's follow the format to write an essay about you; featuring your activities. In nearly all of the essays I wrote to win scholarships, I incorporated information about specific activities in which I was involved. Once you finish, this essay and parts of it (recycling) can probably be used for every essay you write regardless of the question.

If you have an essay you need to write for a scholarship immediately, it will help if you do the following activities first.

- Finish your résumé/activity list if you haven't already. This needs to be done before you begin any essay. Using the information from your résumé/activity list, you should include additional details about your activities to support the main points of your essay.

Scholarship organizations are very impressed by students who are involved in various endeavors beyond typical classroom work. Showing your passion and commitment to certain activities by including more information about your involvement will help you stand out from the crowd of other applicants. Refer to the chapter, "Grades Don't Mean Everything," in *Winning Scholarships for College* for more information and also the "Standing Out With Your Scholarship Application" chapter in this publication.

- Research the organization or company sponsoring the scholarship or award.
- Learn why the scholarship was established and the mission of the organization. If one or more of your activities fit the reasoning behind why the scholarship was established or the organization's mission you may want to highlight this in your essay.
- Understand the question. Think of several ways you might answer and write them down.
- Look at the scholarship application. What do most of the questions focus on: academics, community involvement, etc.? If an organization asks most of its application questions about community involvement, then try to build your essay around activities you do that benefit the community.

Since you are writing a descriptive essay about you or your future career goals, featuring your activities, the next step is to think of three adjectives that describe you. For each adjective, write down an activity that fits with that adjective.

For example, the five-paragraph essay format would now look like the following:

I. INTRODUCTION - ONE PARAGRAPH

    A.   Adjective/Noun 1
    B.   Adjective/Noun 2
    C.   Adjective/Noun 3

II. BODY - THREE PARAGRAPHS

  A. Adjective/Noun 1
    1.   Activity 1
    2.   Activity 2
    3.   Activity 3

  B. Adjective/Noun 2
    1.   Activity 1
    2.   Activity 2
    3.   Activity 3

  C. Adjective/Noun 3
    1.   Activity 1
    2.   Activity 2
    3.   Activity 3

Note: You do not need three activities for each. If you have only two, that's okay.

III. CONCLUSION - ONE PARAGRAPH

    A.   Summarize your adjectives and how they relate to you and your activities. Refer to the future.

As you write about activities in your essay, don't just list them as you did with your résumé/activity list. If you do, the essay is really saying nothing more than you already did. When you write about your activities, you should be answering these questions as part of your essay:

1. What is the activity?
2. Who does the activity benefit?
3. When do you participate in this activity?
4. Where do you participate in this activity?
5. How does this activity benefit you or others?
6. Why are you involved in the activity?

Based on the outline, adjectives, activities, and answers to the above questions, you could begin your essay like the example below, assuming the adjectives you chose were self-motivated, energetic, and compassionate:

When I think of the words self-motivated, energetic, and compassionate, I think of myself. For the past seven years, starting in middle school, into high school and now my first two years in college, I have participated in many activities that reflect these words. More than just words, they really describe who I am and how I feel about life.

For example, in terms of self-motivation, I built a website, Instagram and TikTok page for students interested in getting tutors at our high school and continued maintaining it during college. Building the website and populating it along with Instagram and TikTok with insightful content was a frustrating and challenging task I set for myself. It took me most of the two summers before my freshman year at XYZ University, but I finished it to the amazement of my parents and friends. The website, once completed, became a much-needed reference for students in our community to find tutors and other information to help them in all types of subjects. The Instagram and TikTok content helped with motivation. The website also helped the upper-class students who became tutors make a little money to assist with college expenses and gain experience working with a diverse range of individuals to solve problems. Most importantly, for those who weren't interested in charging, the site helped those who just wanted to aid their peers and apply principles they learned in class.

As a college freshman, I began to show more of my energetic traits by participating in several athletic activities concurrently which really challenged my self-motivation and determination, but most importantly helped me to relearn the value of teamwork and cooperation for all endeavors. I joined the volleyball team. I became involved with student government . . .

The next paragraph would focus on compassionate. The last paragraph would be a summary and conclusion. This essay is an example of a rough draft for a descriptive essay using the adjectives self-motivated, energetic, and compassionate. It still needs work but it's meant to give you an idea of how to structure your essay using the adjectives or nouns you selected and the examples of your activities that could fit the adjectives or nouns you selected.

To get additional information about planning your essays, choosing adjectives, writing about your activities, and writing different types of essays, read *The Scholarship & College Essay Planning Kit.*

Final Words

A primary focus of this book has been to help you realize that no organization gives money without reason. Being aware of those reasons, along with meeting general requirements such as making deadlines, preparing for a dynamic interview, creating an outstanding personal narrative through an essay, composing a flawless and impressive résumé, and thoroughly completing an application give you the best chance of scholarship success. These objectives can be achieved whether you are a high school senior, an undergraduate, or a graduate student. The primary keys to success in finding scholarships are preparation and determination. Therefore, the ideas I have presented in the previous chapters can apply at any stage of the educational process.

Made in the USA
Middletown, DE
27 October 2024

62863500R00056